Faulkner's County: *Yoknapatawpha*

# Faulkner's County: YOKNAPATAWPHA
## by Martin J. Dain

RANDOM HOUSE    NEW YORK

First Printing

Manufactured in the United States of America

Library of Congress catalog card number: 64-17484

Photographic prints by Charles Reiche, Scope Associates

Designed by Erle Yahn

To Passion and Courage:
to Pat
to Dr. and Mrs. James Wesley Silver

*...a Square, the courthouse in its grove*
*the center; quadrangular around it,*
     *the stores...school and church and tavern*
          *and bank and jail each in its ordered place...*

*But above all, the courthouse: the center,*
*the focus, the hub; sitting looming in*
     *the center of the county's circumference*
     *like a single cloud...musing, brooding, symbolic*
*and ponderable, tall as cloud, solid as rock,*
     *dominating all: protector of the weak, judiciate and*
     *curb of the passions and lusts, repository and guardian*
     *of the aspirations and hopes...*

p 27

*Beneath the porticoes of the courthouse*
*and on benches about the green,*
*the city fathers sat and talked and drowsed,*
*in uniform too, here and there.*

*That was the danger, what a man had to*
  *watch against: once you*
    *laid flat on the ground, right away*
    *the earth started in to draw you*
      *back down into it.*

*Father...said time is dead*
*as long as it is being clicked off*
    *by little wheels; only when the clock stops*
        *does time come to life.*

*Tell about the South. What's it*

*like there. What do they do there. Why do they live there. Why do they live at all . . .*

"*War showed de white folks dey cant git along widout
de cullud man. Tromple him in de dus',
but when de trouble bust loose, hit's 'Please, suh, Mr
Cullud Man; right dis way whar de bugle
blowin', Mr Cullud Man; you is de savior of de country.'
And now de cullud race gwine reap de
benefits of de war, and dat soon.*"

...*I'd have wasted a lot of time and trouble before **I** learned that
the best way to take all people, black or white, is to take
them for what they think they are, then leave them alone. **T**hat
was when **I** realised that a nigger is not a person so much
as a form of behaviour; a sort of obverse reflection of the white
people he lives among.*

*. . . safe in Jefferson where life lived too with all its incomprehensible passion and turmoil and grief and fury and despair, but here at six oclock you could close the covers on it and even the weightless hand of a child could put it back among its unfeatured kindred on the quiet eternal shelves and turn the key upon it for the whole and dreamless night . . .*

*. . . he kept an office upstairs above the
Square, where entombed in
dusty filingcases some of the oldest names in
the county—Holston and Sutpen,
Grenier and Beauchamp and Coldfield—
faded year by year among the
bottomless labyrinths of chancery . . .*

. . . *peaceful, with no worries, no need to*
*fight and strive single-handed,*
*not to gain right and justice because they*
*were already lost, but just to defend*
*the principle of them, his rights to them . . .*

*Old Bayard sat tautly back in his chair, his*
*hands on the arms of it, watching the*
*other with his piercing old eyes soberly, a*
*little wistfully; eyes filled with unnamable*
*things, like the eyes of old lions, and intent.*

*. . . if you would peruse in unbroken—ay, overlapping— continuity the history of a community, look not in the church registers and the courthouse records, but beneath the successive layers of calcimine and creosote and whitewash on the walls of the jail, since only in that forcible carceration does man find the idleness in which to compose, in the gross and simple terms of his gross and simple lusts and yearnings, the gross and simple recapitulations of his gross and simple heart . . .*

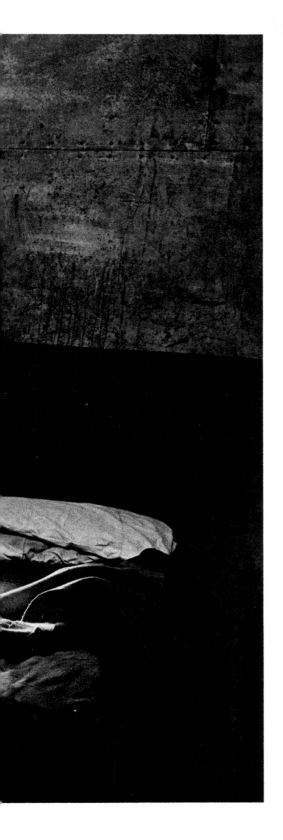

And during all the long weeks while he waited in jail
for his trial, he would stand at the little
window of his cell, his grimed hands gripped among the
bars and his face craned and pressed against
them, to watch a slice of the street . . . which his cousin
would have to cross to come to the jail and
abolish the dream, free him, get him out. "Which is all
I want," he would tell himself. "Jest
to get out of here and go back home and farm.
That dont seem like a heap to ask."

*The jury said "Guilty" and the Judge said "Life" but he didn't hear*
*them. He wasn't listening. In fact, he hadn't been able*
*to listen since that first day when the Judge banged his little wooden*
*hammer on the high desk until he, Mink, dragged his*
*gaze back from the far door of the courtroom to see what in the*
*world the man wanted, and he, the Judge, leaned down*
*across the desk hollering: "You, Snopes! Did you or didn't you kill*
*Jack Houston?" and he, Mink, said, "Dont bother*
*me now. Cant you see I'm busy?"*

"It aint healthy," the
deputy said. "It aint
intended to be. This is the
penitentiary. I cant
imagine no more unhealth
a man can have than
to be locked up inside a
bobwire pen for twenty or
twenty-five years. Besides,
a good unhealthy place
ought to just suit you; you
wont have to stay so long."

"*Man aint really evil, he jest aint got any sense.*"

38

*Only a few of us know that only from homogeneity comes anything of a people or for a people of durable and lasting value— the literature, the art, the science, that minimum of government and police which is the meaning of freedom and liberty, and perhaps most valuable of all a national character worth anything in a crisis—that crisis we shall face someday when we meet an enemy with as many men as we have and as much material as we have and—who knows?—who can even brag and boast as we brag and boast.*

44

"*Years ago we in the South
made our women into ladies.
Then the War came and
made the ladies into ghosts.
So what else can we do, being
gentlemen, but listen to them
being ghosts?*"

*I think that man tries to be better than he thinks he will be.*
*I think that that is his immortality, that he wants to be better, he wants*
*to be braver, he wants to be more honest than he thinks*
*he will be and sometimes he's not, but then suddenly*
*to his own astonishment he is.*

Yes, *he thought,*
between grief and nothing
I will take grief.

*It is not man in the mass who can and will save Man.*
*It is Man himself, created in the image of*
*God so that he shall have the power and the will to*
*choose right from wrong and so be*
*able to save himself because he is worth saving.*

"...'You must struggle, rise. But in order to rise, you must raise the shadow with you. But you can never lift it to your level. I see that now, which I did not see until I came down here. But escape it you cannot. The curse of the black race is God's curse. But the curse of the white race is the black man who will be forever God's chosen own because He once cursed Him.'"

*The preacher had not moved. His arm lay yet across*
*the desk, and he still held that pose while*
*the voice died in sonorous echoes between the walls.*
*It was as different as day and dark from*
*his former tone, with a sad, timbrous quality like an*
*alto horn, sinking into their hearts and*
*speaking there again when it had ceased in*
*fading and cumulate echoes.*
*"Brethren and sisteren," it said again. The preacher*
*removed his arm and he began to walk*
*back and forth before the desk, his hands clasped*
*behind him, a meagre figure, hunched over*
*upon itself like that of one long immured in striving*
*with the implacable earth, "I got the*
*recollection and the blood of the Lamb!"...*
*"Breddren en sistuhn!" His voice rang again, with*
*the horns. He removed his arm and*
*stood erect and raised his hands. "I got de ricklickshun*
*en de blood of de Lamb!" They did not*
*mark just when his intonation, his pronunciation, became*
*negroid, they just sat swaying a little*
*in their seats as the voice took them into itself.*

"I've seed de first en de last," Dilsey said. "Never you mind me."

"First en last whut?" Frony said.

"Never you mind," Dilsey said. "I seed de beginnin, en now I sees de endin."

*. . . that April morning when you woke up and you would think how*
*April was the best, the very best time of all not to have*
*to go to school, until you would think* Except in the fall *with the*
*weather brisk and not-cold at the same time and the*
*trees all yellow and red and you could go hunting all day long; and*
*then you would think* Except in the winter *with the Christmas*
*holidays over and now nothing to look forward to until summer; and*
*you would think how no time is the best time to not*
*have to go to school and so school is a good thing after all because*
*without it there wouldn't be any holidays or vacations.*

*Then one day the old curse of his fathers, the old haughty ancestral pride based not on any value but on an accident of geography, stemmed not from courage and honor but from wrong and shame, descended to him. He did not recognise it then.*

*Because man's hope is in man's freedom.*
  *The basis of the universal truth*
    *which the writer speaks is freedom in*
  *which to hope and believe, since*
    *only in liberty can hope exist—liberty*
*and freedom not given man as a free*
    *gift but as a right and a responsibility to*
*be earned if he deserves it, is worthy*
    *of it, is willing to work for it by means*
  *of courage and sacrifice, and then*
            *to defend it always.*

*But like I said we was all busy or anyway occupied or at least interested, so we could wait. And sho enough, even waiting ends if you can jest wait long enough.*

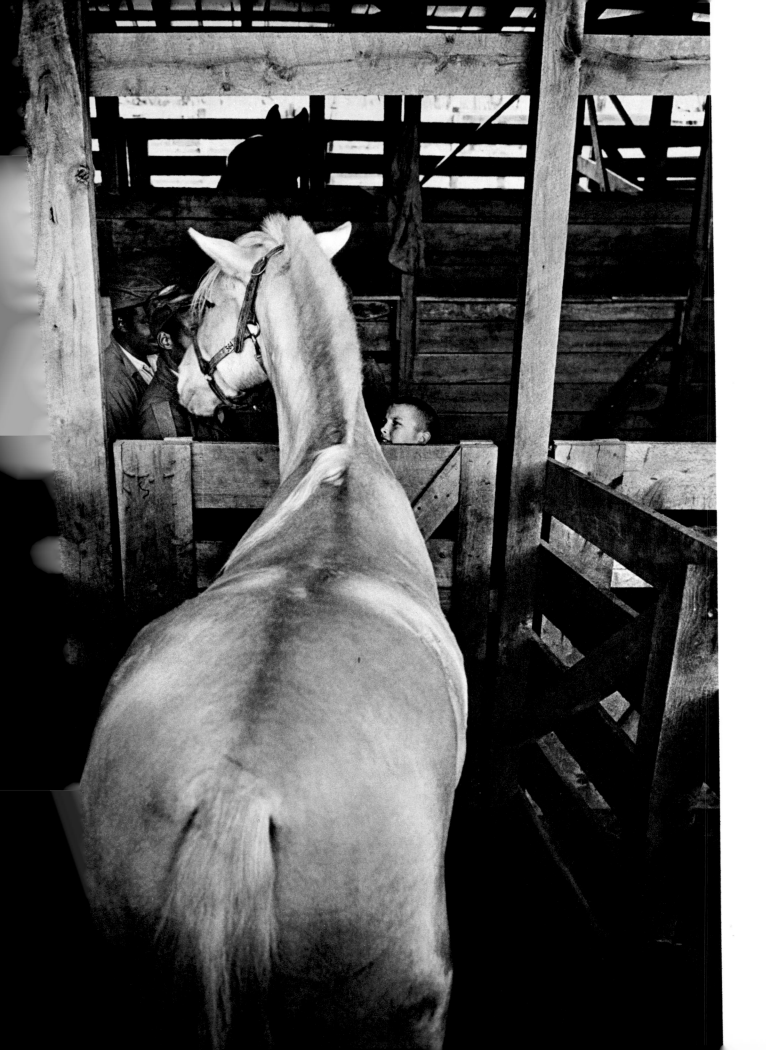

*. . . because Monday was stock-auction day at the*
*sales barns . . . and the men with*
*their stock-trader walking-sticks not even stopping*
*but gone straight across the Square*
*and along the alley to the sales barns to chew tobacco*
*and unlighted cigars from pen to pen*
*amid the ammonia-reek of manure and liniment . . .*

*. . .fear, like so many evil things, comes mainly out of idleness,*
*if you have something to get into tomorrow morning you're too busy*
*to pay much attention to fear. Of course, you have fears, but*
*you have—you don't have time to take them too seriously if you have*
*something to get up to do tomorrow. It don't matter too much*
*what it is . . . and if it's something that you yourself believe is valid . . .*

*. . . thinking remembering how his uncle had said that*
*all man had was time, all that stood*
*between him and the death he feared and abhorred was*
*time yet he spent half of it inventing ways of*
*getting the other half past . . .*

*The settlement had the records; even the simple dispossession of*
*Indians begot in time a minuscule of archive, let alone*
*the normal litter of man's ramshackle confederation against*
*environment—that time and that wilderness—in this case, a meagre,*
*fading, dogeared, uncorrelated, at times illiterate*
*sheaf of land grants and patents and transfers and deeds . . .*

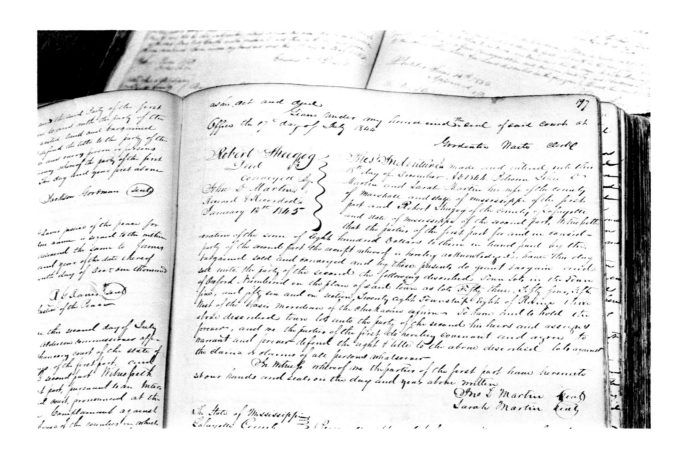

154

one Section of Land situate lying and being in the County of Lafayette and
State of Miss. To wit Section Thirty three, Township Seven, Ranges Three West to the
Pa 23 Meridian. It being the Land to which the said Yock up pa cha
is entitled to under the Treaty of the Twenty Fourth of May Eighteen hundred
and thirty four between the Chickasaw Tribe of Indians and the United
States. To have and to hold the aforesaid Land and Bargained Premises
in fee simple to the only proper use and behoof of the said Goodlow McBuford
his heirs and assigns forever And the said Yock up pa cha covenants to and
with the said G. W. Buford that the before recited Land and bargained premises
as he will warrant and forever defend against the claim or claims of all and
every person or persons whatsoever In testimony whereof the said Yock up
cha has hereunto set his hand and affixed his seal the day and date first
above written.

Wm. C. Mitchell
Thos Hart

Yock up pa cha [seal]

We the undersigned Chiefs do hereby certify that Yock up pa cha the
claimant of Land set forth in the foregoing Deed to G. W. Buford
is capable to manage and take care of his own affairs Given under our
hands this 6th day of December 1836.

Ish te ho te pa [his mark]
Ben Love [mark]

I Benjamin Reynolds Agent for the Chickasaw Nation do hereby
certify that from the best of my knowledge and information the facts set
forth in the foregoing Certificate of the Chiefs are true and that the sum of
Eight Hundred Dollars is a fair Consideration and has been paid by said Bu
ford to the said Yock up pa cha for the Land described in the foregoing Deed
6th December Eighteen Hundred and thirty Six.

Benj. Reynolds
C.A.

The State of Mississippi }
Pontotoc County }

Personally appeared before me Samuel Wilson
Clerk of the Probate Court of said County
C. Mitchell one of the subscribing witnesses to
the foregoing Deed who being first duly sworn deposeth and saith that
he saw Yock up pa cha whose name is subscribed thereto sign seal and
deliver the same to the above named Goodlow McBuford that he subscribed the
same as a witness in presence of said Yock up pa cha and that he saw
Hart the other witness subscribe the same in presence of said Yock up
pa cha and in presence of each other on the day that it bears date
Given under my hand and the seal of said Court at office the 10th
day of December 1836

S. W. Wilson Clk

Pontotoc December 10th 1836

Approved
Wm Carroll
Examining

Jod A Hays
title to Lot in the
Town of Oxford Ms
by Eli Riley

State of
Lafayette

This Indenture
of the County of Lafayette and
Hays of the same County and
in consideration of the two Hund
on fourth on the 14th February and
thereafter the said Realty has bargained
the said Hays a certain parcel
Oxford and County of Lafayette
on the western side of the Sulter S
1650 feet thirty three feet fronty
Street fifty feet to have and to hold
unto him the said Hays his heirs and
said his heir executors and admin
Hays his heirs and assigns the title
claim or demand of any person of

Test
R. Isselyn

The State of Mississippi
Lafayette County

A Hays who acknowledged the
Deed for the purposes therein conta
office at Oxford November

[seal]

Wilson & Moore
Bond for title to
the Lot in Oxford Miss

State of
Lafayette

Oxford

Know all men by these presents
C Mitchell of the County of Miss
Bargained and Sold unto
County of Hardeman and S
& in the Town of Oxford Mis
ca this day their Notes to the said
One Note for Eighty Three doll
day of February 1837. One for one
payable on the Twenty first day of
and thirty seven twenty six
payable the 15th day of February
as upon said I covenant to and w

*The house was a gutted ruin rising gaunt and stark*
*out of a grove of unpruned cedar trees.*
*It was a landmark, known as the Old Frenchman*
*place, built before the Civil War; a*
*plantation house set in the middle of a tract of land;*
*of cotton fields and gardens and lawns*
*long since gone back to jungle, which the people of the*
*neighborhood had been pulling down*
*piecemeal for firewood for fifty years or digging with*
*secret and sporadic optimism for the gold*
*which the builder was reputed to have buried somewhere*
*about the place when Grant came through*
*the county on his Vicksburg campaign.*

*"... I mind I used to think that hope was about all folks had, only now I'm
beginning to believe that that's about all anybody needs—jest hope ..."*

*'It is because a fellow is more afraid of the trouble*
*he might have than he ever is of the*
*trouble he's already got. He'll cling to trouble he's*
*used to before he'll risk a change . . .'*

*And when **I** think about that, **I** think that if nothing*
*but being married will help a man,*
*he's durn nigh hopeless. But **I** reckon Cora's right*
*when she says the reason the **L**ord had*
*to create women is because man dont know his*
*own good when he sees it.*

*Because they, Negroes, when the problems
are not from the passions of want
and ignorance and fear—gambling, drink—
but are of simple humanity, are a
gentle and tender people, a little more so
than white people because they have had
to be; a little wiser in their dealings with
white people than white people
are with them, because they have had to
survive in a minority.*

*"Then you're a fool," I says.*

*"Well," he says, "I dont spute dat neither. Ef dat uz a crime,
all chain-gangs wouldn't be black."*

*. . . that blending of childlike and ready incompetence and paradoxical*
*reliability that tends and protects them it loves . . . robs*
*them steadily and evades responsibility and obligations by means*
*too barefaced to be called subterfuge . . . and withal a fond*
*and unflagging tolerance for whitefolks' vagaries like that of a*
*grandparent for unpredictable and troublesome children . . .*

*"That we have got to make the
    white people need us first. In the
old days your people did
    need us, in your economy if not
    your culture, to make your
cotton and tobacco and indigo.
But that was the wrong need,
    bad and evil in itself. So it
couldn't last. It had to go . . ."*

*"I works to suit de man whut pays me
     Sat'dy night," he says. "When I
does dat, it dont leave me a whole lot of time
  to please other folks . . . Aint nobody
     works much in dis country cep de boll-weevil,
      noways," he says.*

*"There aren't any morals," Stevens said. "People just
do the best they can."
"The pore sons of bitches," Ratliff said.
"The poor sons of bitches," Stevens said.*

*"Tomorrow is just another name for today."*
*. . . "But tomorrow is today also."*
*"Yao. Tomorrow is today."*

*. . . until was it any wonder that a man would*
*look at that inimical irreconcilable*
*square of dirt to which he was bound and*
*chained for the rest of his life, and say*
*to it:* You got me, you'll wear me out because
you are stronger than me since
I'm jest bone and flesh. I cant leave you
because I cant afford to, and you know it.

*That's the one trouble with this
country: everything, weather,
all, hangs on too long. Like our rivers,
our land: opaque, slow, violent;
shaping and creating the life of man
in its implacable and brooding image.*

*. . . then it would be the sharp,*

*subtly exciting odor of fermentation and of boiling molasses.*

"... The woods and fields
he ravages and the game he
devastates will be the consequence
and signature of his crime
and guilt, and his punishment.—
Bed time," I say; then
to young Ash: "Breakfast
at four oclock, Ash. We want
meat on the ground by sunup."

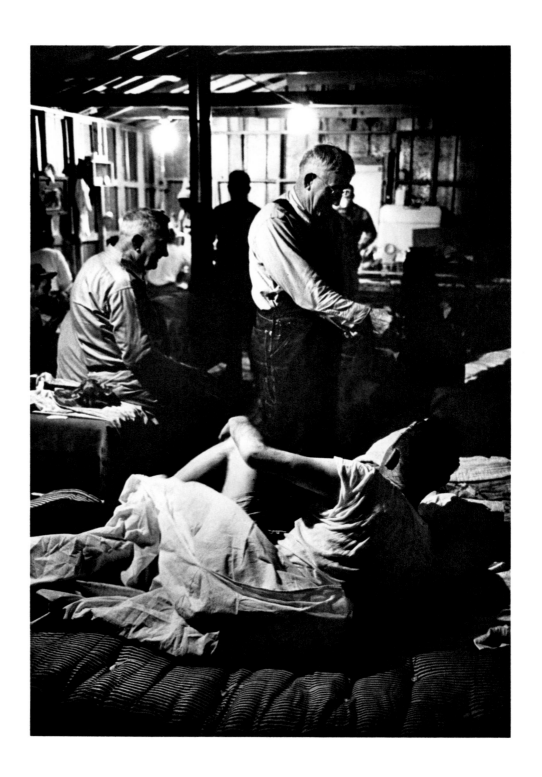

*. . . the same solitude, the same*
*loneliness through which*
*frail and timorous man had*
*merely passed without altering it,*
*leaving no mark nor scar, which*
*looked exactly as it must have*
*looked when the first ancestor*
*of **Sam Father's** **Chickasaw***
*predecessors crept into it . . .*

*In the old days we came in wagons: the guns, the*
*bedding, the dogs, the food, the whisky . . .*
*There had been bear then. A man shot a doe or a*
*fawn as quickly as he did a buck . . .*
*Now we go in cars, driving faster and faster each year*
*because the roads are better and the distance*
*greater, the Big Woods where game still runs drawing*
*yearly inward as my life is doing . . .*

*Oh yes, he would think; me too. I've been too busy all my life trying not to waste any living, to have time left to die.*

*This land, said the old hunter. No wonder the ruined woods I used to know dont cry for retribution.*
*The very people who destroyed them will accomplish their revenge.*

*Our tragedy today is a general and universal physical fear
so long sustained by now that we can even bear it. There
are no longer problems of the spirit . . . He must teach himself
that the basest of all things is to be afraid; and, teaching himself
that, forget it forever, leaving no room in his workshop
for anything but the old verities and truths of the heart, the old
universal truths lacking which any story is ephemeral and doomed—
love and honor and pity and pride and compassion and
sacrifice . . . I believe that man will not merely endure: he will prevail.
He is immortal, not because he alone among creatures has an
inexhaustible voice, but because he has a soul, a spirit capable of
compassion and sacrifice and endurance.*

"It is any man's privilege to destroy himself, so long as he
does not injure anyone else, so long as he
lives to and of himself . . ."

His head was lifted a little
in that gesture of haughty pride
    which repeated itself generation
after generation with a
    fateful fidelity, his back to the
world and his carven eyes
    gazing out across the valley
where his railroad ran, and the
    blue changeless hills beyond, and
beyond that, the ramparts of
    infinity itself. . . . the bold
carving of the letters was bleared
with mold, yet still decipherable:

COLONEL JOHN SARTORIS, C. S. A.
1823                                                    1876

Billy 11

*I'm inclined to think that
the only peace man knows is—he
    says, Why good gracious,
        yesterday I was happy. That at
the moment he's too busy.
        That maybe peace is only a
    condition in retrospect, when the
        subconscious has got rid of
the gnats and the tacks and the
        broken glass in experience
and has left only the peaceful
        pleasant things—that was peace.
    Maybe peace is not is, but was.*

148

*Because no battle is ever won he said. They are not even fought.*
*The field only reveals to man his own*
*folly and despair, and victory is an illusion of philosophers and fools.*

*"Think of all that has happened here, on this earth. All the blood hot*
*and strong for living, pleasuring, that has soaked*
*back into it. For grieving and suffering too, of course, but still getting*
*something out of it for all that, getting a lot out of it,*
*because after all you dont have to continue to bear what you believe is*
*suffering; you can always choose to stop that, put an end*
*to that. And even suffering and grieving is better than nothing; there*
*is only one thing worse than not being alive,*
*and that's shame. But you cant be alive forever, and you always*
*wear out life long before you have exhausted the possibilities*
*of living. And all that must be somewhere; all that could not have been*
*invented and created just to be thrown away..."*

"...Now *I want you to tell me just one thing more. Why do you
hate the South?*"
"*I dont hate it,*" Quentin said, *quickly, at once, immediately;*
"*I dont hate it,*" *he said.* I dont hate it *he thought, panting in the cold
air, the iron New England dark;* I dont. I dont!
I dont hate it! I dont hate it!

# Explanatory Notes

The personality of William Faulkner will remain an enigma, but the country around him, our world, is as clear as one is willing to see. Beneath the superficial reality of a place, lie the thoughts and actions of men, by which we shall be able to discern the noble from the ignoble, the courageous from the cowardly, the moral from the self-righteous, the individuals from the mob, and the leaders from the followers. Faulkner's county is not much different, I think, from any place else on Earth. The problems of his people are universal problems. Their tragedies and their humor evoke our compassion and our understanding.

On the preceding pages I have tried to evoke some of this world. It is by no means all. There is much of contemporary life that is not shown; such as the housing developments and the modern glass store fronts. Although the photographs illustrate Yoknapatawpha County, a small world, that world is yours, your own backyard. "Endure and prevail," he said.

My deepest thanks to those who have helped me with this book, especially the people of Oxford, Mississippi.

MARTIN J. DAIN

*Page 7*  Quote from *Requiem for a Nun.*

8-9  Early evening in August, the sun still hot and the air heavy. The statue faces south and behind, the Courthouse (rebuilt about 1871, having been burned in 1864 by General A. H. Smith's troops), in Oxford, the county seat of Lafayette County, Mississippi.

10-11  Around the Square, the town begins to get busy. It is Saturday.

11  Quote from *Sartoris.*

12  In the shade of trees by the Courthouse, a man finds peace in the August heat.

13  Top: Transient fruit and vegetable markets surround the Courthouse, especially on Saturdays.
Bottom: This is the base of the statue of the Confederate soldier.

13  Quotes from *The Mansion* and *The Sound and the Fury.*

14-15  Summer and winter, men sit in the cool (or warm) hall of the Courthouse, and watch and wait and talk. This is great storytelling country.

14-15  Quote from *Absalom, Absalom!*

16  On Saturdays, country and town folk gather about the Square. It is the shopping and general meeting day. Many just watch and wait. There are no marked boundaries, but tradition has established that Negroes gather at specific parts of the Square.

17  These enticing signs appear in front of the Federal Building, which houses the post office. It is the northeast corner of the Square.

17  Quote from *Sartoris.*

18-19  In an alley to the side of Phil Stone's law offices, on the fringe of the Square, are a few Negro stores. This restaurant is one of them. The county is "dry."

19  Quote from *The Sound and the Fury.*

20-21  The northwest (bottom) and the southeast (top) corners of the Square.

22  Quote from *The Sound and the Fury.*

23  Looking south from the Courthouse. An early December evening.

24-27  In and about the law offices of Judge John Wesley Thompson Falkner II, Faulkner's uncle, now dead.

25  Quote from *The Sound and the Fury.*

27  Quotes from *The Mansion* and *Sartoris.*

28-31  The jail and a former deputy sheriff. The jail, built around 1870, was on the top floor; the bottom floor housed the deputy and his family. This jail was demolished in 1962, and a modern one stands in its place. On my first visit the walls were covered with graffiti, some vulgar, some noble. The walls were partially cleaned before my second visit.

28  Quote from *Requiem for a Nun.*

31  Quote from *The Mansion.*

32  Quote from *The Mansion.*

33  The judge is swearing in a grand jury to investigate and perhaps indict those responsible for the troubles in Oxford and at the University, during the matriculation of James Meredith, in October, 1962.

34-37  The state penitentiary at Parchman, about 100 miles southwest of Oxford.

35  Quote from *The Mansion.*

38  A bootlegger's grocery across the county line provides hard liquor and beer for those who do not wish to drive to Memphis, 75 miles away. Some counties of Mississippi sell beer. Lafayette voted dry in spite of Mr. Faulkner's urging in his beer

broadside in September, 1950, of which he printed and distributed 1500 copies.

38 Quote from *The Mansion*.

39 Quote from *Intruder in the Dust*.

40 Top: Phil Stone, erudite lawyer and friend of Faulkner's youth and mature years. Faulkner's trilogy, *Snopes*, is dedicated to him.
Bottom: Professor James W. Silver has taught history at the University since 1936 and has been a friend of the Faulkners since then. Courageous and unequivocal, he has led a liberal group, and this book is respectfully dedicated to him and his wife.

41 Top: The Mayor of Oxford, Richard Elliott. He runs a funeral parlor and two jewelry stores.
Bottom: Now dead, Dr. Christopher Longest was president of the First National Bank of Oxford, and had been a professor at the University.

42 Top: In his studio are photographer "Colonel" J. R. Cofield (left) and Mack Reed (right), old friends of Faulkner's.
Bottom left: The Rector of St. Peter's Episcopal Church, Reverend Duncan M. Gray, Jr. He preached Faulkner's brief funeral service.
Bottom right: Dr. Felix Linder still keeps an office though he is semi-retired. He is a boyhood chum of Faulkner's.

43 Twins Eph and Ed Lowe, one-time county surveyors, and connoisseurs of vintage autos. Their father helped Faulkner build his first airplane. The plane was pushed off the side of a hill. It did not fly or glide. Faulkner was unhurt.

44 Top: John Wesley Thompson Faulkner III, who died in 1963, was William's younger brother. He was a novelist and a primitive painter. The painting in the photograph shows a balloon ascension in the Square during a county fair.
Bottom: Jerrold "Red" Brite was one of Faulkner's hunting companions.

45 Top: John Cullen, hunter, local newspaper columnist, hog raiser, and great storyteller.
Bottom: J. H. Moody owns a good bottomland farm bordering on the Yocona River.

46 Top: Mrs. O. A. Shaw, sole proprietress of a brick antebellum mansion. She is spiritedly independent and courageous.
Bottom: Mrs. Maud Brown is a local church historian who recognized Faulkner as a poet in the early twenties. Faulkner once presented a story to her invalid daughter.

46 Quote from *Absalom, Absalom!*

47 Bill Evans, a retired farmer and carpenter and painter. He has been hunting for thirty years. He is 65 years old.

47 Quote from *Faulkner in the University*.

48-51 Reverend W. N. Redmond, of Burns Methodist Church, is also principal of a Negro elementary school in Abbeville. Here he gives Communion to the sick and the aged. A friend of James Meredith, Reverend Redmond met regularly with white ministers during the integration troubles.

51 Quote from *The Wild Palms*.

52-55 College Hill Presbyterian Church is a classic beauty a few miles northwest of Oxford. John Faulkner says that his brother was married in this church. The scenes here are of an adult Bible class, hymn singing, and the blackboard in a Sunday school classroom.

52 Quote from an address to the graduating class of University High School, Oxford, Mississippi.

54 Quote from *Light in August*.

56-61 Mt. Hope Baptist Church. The preacher came about forty miles to preach the Sunday service at this small rural church. With bad weather and muddy roads, these people waited hours for him to arrive.

56 Quote from *The Sound and the Fury*.

61 Quote from *The Sound and the Fury*.

62 Waiting for a school bus in April in the hamlet of Tula, near the southern boundary of the county.

62 Quote from *The Town*.

63-65 Yocona Vocational School, Yocona, Mississippi, about 17 miles southeast of Oxford. The name derives from YOKNAPATAWFA and is pronounced "Yawkny."

66-68 A new elementary school in Abbeville, about 15 miles north of Oxford.

69 Quote from *Go Down, Moses*.

70-71 Two boys, one Negro and one white, play together.

72 Mr. M. R. Hall (bottom), a blacksmith for whom there is not much work in a modern community. Sometimes wagon wheels from as far away as eighty miles are sent to him for repair.

72 Quote from *Faulkner at Nagano*.

73 Leslie Oliver (top), 76 years old, is now a miller. As a boy he worked in an ice plant owned by Faulkner's father. Here they sit at the blacksmith's shop listening to a football game.

73 Quote from *The Town*.

74-75 Auction of stock takes place every Monday on the outskirts of Oxford. This palomino did not sell.

75 Quote from *Intruder in the Dust*.

76-81 Tommy Bounds is an itinerant salesman for Watkins Products. His routes take him to the limits of the county deep in the countryside. He sells a variety of items: liniment, spices, toilet articles, insecticides, vitamins for animals and people. His ebullient personality makes him universally welcome. Bounds has about 450 customers and has been selling for twenty years. There is no longer an itinerant sewing-machine salesman.

76 Quote from *Faulkner in the University*.

81 Quote from *Intruder in the Dust*.

82 Mr. Shegog bought the land and built the house that became Faulkner's.

82 Quote from *Requiem for a Nun*.

83 An early land transaction between white men and Chickasaw Indians, dated 1836.

84 An abandoned ante-bellum house, the Shipp place, deep in the country. Not even squatters live there any more.

84 Quote from *Sanctuary*.

85 The skeleton of a dog in an abandoned shed.

86-89 Rural Mississippi.

87    Quote from *The Mansion*.

88    Quote from *Light in August*.

90    The postmistress of Paris, on the southern border of the county.

91    About 15 miles southwest of Oxford, at the fork of two dirt roads, one will find this suggestive scene.

90    Quote from *As I Lay Dying*.

92-97    More rural scenes.

94    Quote from *The Mansion*.

96    Quote from *The Sound and the Fury*.

98-101    An ante-bellum house known as the Jones-Miller place now inhabited by Mrs. Book and her family, southwest of Oxford. The little boy's crying was not understandable until it was explained to me that he was afraid of white men.

99    Quote from *The Sound and the Fury*.

102    The flag was drying in the sun, having been washed for the local school. The woman draws water from the well.

103-108    Picking late cotton. The fields were too wet for mechanical pickers, the cotton is poor.

103    Quote from *The Mansion*.

109    Cotton dust blown from the exhaust system of a cotton gin covers the trees and sidewalks and bushes.

110-111    The raw cotton is sucked up from the wagon bed to begin the ginning process.

111    Quote from *The Sound and the Fury*.

112    Portraits at a cotton gin.

113    Quote from *The Mansion*.

114-115    In a November evening, this man returns to his home in his cotton wagon. Mule-drawn vehicles are becoming rare.

116    A Wells family portrait, photographed about 1905. It is the same plot of land as the photograph on page 117, and almost the same house.

116    Quote from *Red Leaves*.

117-123    Mr. E. W. Wells, his wife and sisters, daughters and a grandson in 1962. He has 156 acres of land, some of it badly eroded; but with government help, he is trying to save it. In 1962, his 8½ acres of cotton yielded 10 bales. He harvests his crops with the help of his son-in-law.

122    Quote from *The Mansion*.

124    Near Hurricane Landing in April. The area is flooded by waters overflowing from nearby Sardis Lake.

125    Fishing on the Tallahatchie, the northern boundary of the county.

125    Quote from *As I Lay Dying*.

126-127    Hurricane (pronounced Harrykin) Landing in November. This area is under water in the spring.

128-130    Making sorghum molasses in the early fall—a craft becoming rare.

129-130    Quote from *Sartoris*.

131-141    Deer hunts occur in Thanksgiving and Christmas weeks, and now one must travel 165 miles into the Delta. There are no longer any bear. At seven in the morning the camp boss blows his horn, rousing the deer. The dogs trail and the men, waiting in their solitary stands since sunup, watch for a buck. One may celebrate a kill with some matured corn.

131-41    Quotes from *Big Woods*.

142    Quote from the Nobel Prize speech.

143-153    The photographs of William C. Faulkner were taken at his home, Rowan Oak, in March, 1962, and are the last ones taken of him in Mississippi.

144    In the cemetery at Ripley, Mississippi, is this monument of Faulkner's illustrious great-grandfather, the Old Colonel, William Clark Falkner. It overlooks the railroad he built. Legends of his times are still told by natives of this area. Colonel Falkner wrote a best-selling novel, *The White Rose of Memphis*.

144    Quotes from *Light in August* and *Sartoris*.

145    Colonel Falkner stabbed Hindman to death after Hindman's pistol had twice failed to fire, in an argument the basis of which is still obscure. This grave is in the Hindman family plot, 1½ miles east of Ripley. Falkner himself was shot and killed by a former business associate in 1889.

146    Top: William Cuthbert Faulkner, aged 11 months.
Bottom: Left to right, standing—Murry, 8 years; Sallie Murry Wilkins, 8 years; William, 10 years; and seated, Johncie, 6 years. September, 1907. Photo courtesy of Mrs. Sallie Murry Wilkins Williams.

147    Left: William Faulkner on the right with his cousin, J. W. T. Falkner IV. Photo courtesy of Mrs. J. W. T. Falkner III, and taken by her in 1910 or 1911.
Right: William with his arms around John with Murry holding John's hand, taken about 1905. Photo courtesy of Mrs. Sallie Murry Wilkins Williams.

147    Quote from *Faulkner in the University*.

148    Top: Taken about 1905 in front of the first Falkner home in Oxford, after moving from Ripley. William Cuthbert Faulkner on spotted pony. Sallie Murry Wilkins, first cousin to the boys, sitting on steps with Murry Charles, and Johncie holding the small pony. Photo courtesy of Mrs. Sallie Murry Wilkins Williams.
Bottom: Faulkner's mother, Maud, painted her son after he returned from flight training in Canada, in 1918.

149    Faulkner's study at Rowan Oak. He painted on the wall an outline of his novel *A Fable*.

149    Quote from *The Sound and the Fury*.

150    The fence gate was newly made by Mr. Faulkner and is non-sag. The dog was one of many around the yard.

151-153    Faulkner leads a favorite horse into the barn. The barn is hand-hewn, built about 1840.

152    Quote from *Big Woods*.

154    The small house at Faulkner's farm about 15 miles northeast of Oxford.

155    Faulkner's ante-bellum house, Rowan Oak.

155    Quote from *Absalom, Absalom!*

---

Note: All photographs were taken with Leicas on Kodak film.

## DATE DUE